IN JESUS YOU ARE
for kids

UNDERSTANDING YOUR
IDENTITY IN CHRIST

LOVEGODGREATLY.COM

A Word to Parents

This book grew out of a desire to
provide a companion study journal
for children to use alongside the
In Jesus You Are adult study journal and
book.

Love God Greatly is dedicated to making
God's Word available to our beautiful
community of women... and now, women
have the opportunity to share God's Word
with children through this study uniquely
crafted for young hearts.

CONTENTS

07 INTRODUCTION

08 READING PLAN

11 YOUR GOALS

12 WEEK 1

30 WEEK 2

50 WEEK 3

68 WEEK 4

INTRODUCTION

IN JESUS YOU ARE

WHAT IS YOUR IDENTITY?

Identity is how a person or thing is defined, either how it defines itself or how others define it. We each have an identity, one that is unique. Sometimes we define our identity by our family, friends, likes, dislikes, activities, or where we live. Our thoughts, words, and actions all help define our identity. While we all have a distinct identity, sometimes it can be hard to know what that is.

Without knowing our true identity, we cannot live how we were made to live. In Jesus, we have a secure, unchanging identity. He came to earth to save us from our sins, dying on the cross and raising to life, defeating death and sin forever. Because of His sacrifice for us, we have a new identity: we are His children.

When we believe in Jesus and choose to follow Him, we are made new. Because Jesus has taken on the consequences of our sin for us, we are able to live without guilt and shame. He has removed our sin and made us new. We are forgiven of all our sin and restored to a perfect relationship with God. We are delivered from evil and forever secure. We will spend eternity with Him!

Though it can be hard to understand, especially when we live in a world that wants to give us its own identity, our identity in Christ never changes. Through Christ, God has chosen us to be His children. He has redeemed us from sin through Christ's sacrifice. He promises to never leave us. If we are God's children, if we have chosen to follow Jesus, we are forever secure.

As you learn about your identity in Christ, ask God to show you how much He loves you. Ask Him to show you who you are in Him, and ask Him to help you believe His truth. Together, let's learn about who we are in Jesus.

READING PLAN

WEEK 1

Monday – I Am A New Creation
Read: 2 Corinthians 5:17; Colossians 3:9–10
SOAP: 2 Corinthians 5:17

Tuesday – I Am Forgiven
Read: Ephesians 1:7–8; 1 John 1:9
SOAP: Ephesians 1:7

Wednesday – I Am Righteous
Read: Romans 5:1–2
SOAP: Romans 5:1–2

Thursday – I Am Delivered
Read: Psalm 107:1–3; Isaiah 43:1–3; Romans 8:1–4
SOAP: Isaiah 43:1

Friday – I Am Sealed
Read: 2 Corinthians 1:21–22
SOAP: 2 Corinthians 1:21–22

WEEK 2

Monday – I Am Rescued
Read: John 3:16–17; Colossians 1:11–14; Hebrews 2:14–15
SOAP: Colossians 1:13

Tuesday – I Am Saved
Read: Romans 5:8–10; Ephesians 2:1–5
SOAP: Ephesians 2:4–5

Wednesday – I Am Free
Read: John 8:36; 2 Corinthians 3:17
SOAP: John 8:36

Thursday – I Am Loved
Read: 1 John 4:10–19; Romans 8:35–39
SOAP: 1 John 4:10

Friday – I Am Received
Read: Romans 15:7–9
SOAP: Romans 15:7

WEEK 3

Monday – I Am Adopted
Read: Ephesians 1:5–6; Colossians 1:12–13
SOAP: Ephesians 1:5

Tuesday – I Am A Child of God
Read: John 1:12; 1 John 3:1–2
SOAP: John 1:12

Wednesday – I Am Chosen
Read: Ephesians 1:4; 1 Peter 2:9
SOAP: 1 Peter 2:9

Thursday – I Am A Citizen of Heaven
Read: Ephesians 2:19; Philippians 3:20
SOAP: Philippians 3:20

Friday – I Am Known by God
Read: Psalm 139:1–3; 1 Corinthians 8:3
SOAP: Psalm 139:1

WEEK 4

Monday – I Am Intentionally Made
Read: Psalm 139:13–18
SOAP: Psalm 139:13–14

Tuesday – I Am Blessed
Read: Numbers 6:24–26; 2 Corinthians 9:8–10; Ephesians 1:3
SOAP: Ephesians 1:3

Wednesday – I Am Equipped
Read: Ephesians 2:10; 2 Timothy 3:16–17
SOAP: Ephesians 2:10

Thursday – I Am Empowered
Read: 1 Corinthians 12:4–11; 2 Corinthians 12:9; Philippians 4:13
SOAP: Philippians 4:13

Friday – I Am A Conqueror
Read: 1 John 4:4
SOAP: 1 John 4:4

YOUR GOALS

We believe it's important to write out goals for this study. Take some time now and write three goals you would like to focus on as you begin to rise each day and dig into God's Word. Make sure and refer back to these goals throughout the next weeks to help you stay focused. You can do it!

1.

2.

3.

Signature:

Date:

PRAYER

WRITE DOWN YOUR PRAYER REQUESTS AND PRAISES FOR EACH DAY.

Prayer focus for this week:
Spend time praying for your family members.

MONDAY

TUESDAY

WEDNESDAY

THURSDAY

FRIDAY

WEEK 1

So then, if anyone is in Christ, he is a new creation; what is old has passed away—look, what is new has come!

2 Corinthians 5:17

_____

SCRIPTURE FOR WEEK 1

MONDAY

2 Corinthians 5:17

So then, if anyone is in Christ, he is a new creation; what is old has passed away—look, what is new has come!

Colossians 3:9–10

Do not lie to one another since you have put off the old man with its practices 10 and have been clothed with the new man that is being renewed in knowledge according to the image of the one who created it.

TUESDAY

Ephesians 1:7–8

In him we have redemption through his blood, the forgiveness of our offenses, according to the riches of his grace 8 that he lavished on us in all wisdom and insight.

1 John 1:9

But if we confess our sins, he is faithful and righteous, forgiving us our sins and cleansing us from all unrighteousness.

WEDNESDAY

Romans 5:1–2

Therefore, since we have been declared righteous by faith, we have peace with God through our Lord Jesus Christ, 2 through whom we have also obtained access into this grace in which we stand, and we rejoice in the hope of God's glory.

THURSDAY

Psalm 107:1–3

Give thanks to the Lord, for he is good,
and his loyal love endures.
2 Let those delivered by the Lord speak out,

those whom he delivered from the power of the enemy,
3 and gathered from foreign lands,
from east and west,
from north and south.

Isaiah 43:1–3

Now, this is what the LORD says,
the one who created you, O Jacob,
and formed you, O Israel:
"Don't be afraid, for I will protect you.
I call you by name, you are mine.
2 When you pass through the waters, I am with you;
when you pass through the streams, they will not overwhelm you.
When you walk through the fire, you will not be burned;
the flames will not harm you.
3 For I am the LORD your God,
the Holy One of Israel, your deliverer.
I have handed over Egypt as a ransom price,
Ethiopia and Seba in place of you.

Romans 8:1–4

There is therefore now no condemnation for those who are in Christ Jesus. 2 For the law of the life–giving Spirit in Christ Jesus has set you free from the law of sin and death. 3 For God achieved what the law could not do because it was weakened through the flesh. By sending his own Son in the likeness of sinful flesh and concerning sin, he condemned sin in the flesh, 4 so that the righteous requirement of the law may be fulfilled in us, who do not walk according to the flesh but according to the Spirit.

FRIDAY

2 Corinthians 1:21–22

But it is God who establishes us together with you in Christ and who anointed us, 22 who also sealed us and gave us the Spirit in our hearts as a down payment.

MONDAY

Read:
2 Corinthians 5:17; Colossians 3:9–10

SOAP:
2 Corinthians 5:17

1. Write out today's **SCRIPTURE** passage.

_____

_____

_____

_____

_____

_____

_____

_____

_____

_____

2. On the blank page to the right, **DRAW** or **WRITE** what this passage means to you.

3. My **PRAYER** for today:

_____

_____

_____

_____

_____

TUESDAY

Read:
Ephesians 1:7–8; 1 John 1:9
SOAP:
Ephesians 1:7

1. Write out today's **SCRIPTURE** passage.

_____

_____

_____

_____

_____

_____

_____

_____

_____

_____

2. On the blank page to the right, **DRAW** or **WRITE** what this passage means to you.

3. My **PRAYER** for today:

_____

_____

_____

_____

_____

WEDNESDAY

Read:
Romans 5:1–2
SOAP:
Romans 5:1–2

1. Write out today's **SCRIPTURE** passage.

_____

_____

_____

_____

_____

_____

_____

_____

_____

_____

2. On the blank page to the right, **DRAW** or **WRITE** what this passage means to you.

3. My **PRAYER** for today:

_____

_____

_____

_____

_____

_____

THURSDAY

Read:
Psalm 107:1–3; Isaiah 43:1–3; Romans 8:1–4

SOAP:
Isaiah 43:1

1. Write out today's **SCRIPTURE** passage.

_____

_____

_____

_____

_____

_____

_____

_____

_____

_____

2. On the blank page to the right, **DRAW** or **WRITE** what this passage means to you.

3. My **PRAYER** for today:

_____

_____

_____

_____

_____

FRIDAY

Read:
2 Corinthians 1:21–22

SOAP:
2 Corinthians 1:21–22

1. Write out today's **SCRIPTURE** passage.

_____

_____

_____

_____

_____

_____

_____

_____

_____

_____

2. On the blank page to the right, **DRAW** or **WRITE** what this passage means to you.

3. My **PRAYER** for today:

_____

_____

_____

_____

_____

_____

THIS WEEK I LEARNED...

USE THE SPACE BELOW TO DRAW A PICTURE OR WRITE ABOUT WHAT YOU LEARNED THIS WEEK FROM YOUR TIME IN GOD'S WORD.

FILL IN THE BLANK

READ 2 CORINTHIANS 5:17 AND USE IT TO FILL IN THE MISSING WORDS

So then, if anyone is in Christ, he is a new creation; what
is old has passed away—look, what is new has come!
2 Corinthians 5:17

So then, if ＿＿＿＿＿＿ is
in ＿＿＿＿ , he is a ＿＿＿
creation; what is ＿＿ has
passed away—＿＿＿＿ ,
what is ＿＿ has come!

PRAYER

WRITE DOWN YOUR PRAYER REQUESTS
AND PRAISES FOR EACH DAY.

Prayer focus for this week:
Spend time praying for your country.

MONDAY

TUESDAY

WEDNESDAY

THURSDAY

FRIDAY

WEEK 2

But God, being rich in mercy, because of his great love with which he loved us, even though we were dead in offenses, made us alive together with Christ—by grace you are saved!

Ephesians 2:4-5

SCRIPTURE FOR WEEK 2

MONDAY

John 3:16–17

16 For this is the way God loved the world: He gave his one and only Son, so that everyone who believes in him will not perish but have eternal life.17 For God did not send his Son into the world to condemn the world, but that the world should be saved through him.

Colossians 1:11–14

being strengthened with all power according to his glorious might for the display of all patience and steadfastness, joyfully 12 giving thanks to the Father who has qualified you to share in the saints' inheritance in the light. 13 He delivered us from the power of darkness and transferred us to the kingdom of the Son he loves, 14 in whom we have redemption, the forgiveness of sins.

Hebrews 2:14–15

Therefore, since the children share in flesh and blood, he likewise shared in their humanity, so that through death he could destroy the one who holds the power of death (that is, the devil), 15 and set free those who were held in slavery all their lives by their fear of death.

TUESDAY

Romans 5:8–10

But God demonstrates his own love for us, in that while we were still sinners, Christ died for us. 9 Much more then, because we have now been declared righteous by his blood, we will be saved through him from God's wrath. 10 For if while we were enemies we were reconciled to God through the death of his Son, how much more, since we have been reconciled, will we be saved by his life?

Ephesians 2:1–5

And although you were dead in your offenses and sins, 2 in which you formerly lived according to this world's present path, according to the ruler of the domain of the air, the ruler of the spirit that is now energizing the sons of disobedience, 3 among whom all of us also formerly lived out our lives in the cravings of our flesh, indulging the desires of the flesh and the mind, and were by nature children of wrath even as the rest…4 But God, being rich in mercy, because of his great love with which he loved us, 5 even though we were dead in offenses, made us alive together with Christ—by grace you are saved!—

WEDNESDAY

John 8:36

So if the son sets you free, you will be really free.

2 Corinthians 3:17

Now the LORD is the Spirit, and where the Spirit of the LORD is present, there is freedom.

THURSDAY

1 John 4:10–19

In this is love: not that we have loved God, but that he loved us and sent his Son to be the atoning sacrifice for our sins.

11 Dear friends, if God so loved us, then we also ought to love one another. 12 No one has seen God at any time. If we love one another, God resides in us, and his love is perfected in us. 13 By this we know that we reside in God and he in us: in that he has given us of his Spirit. 14 And we have seen and testify that the Father has sent the Son to be the Savior of the world.

15 If anyone confesses that Jesus is the Son of God, God resides in him and he in God. 16 And we have come to know and to believe the love that God has in us. God is love, and the one who resides in love resides in God, and God resides in him. 17 By this love is perfected with us, so that we may have confidence in the day of judgment, because just as Jesus is, so also are we in this world. 18 There is no fear in love, but perfect love drives out fear, because fear has to do with punishment. The one who fears punishment has not been perfected in love. 19 We love because he loved us first.

Romans 8:35–39

Who will separate us from the love of Christ? Will trouble, or distress, or persecution, or famine, or nakedness, or danger, or sword? 36 As it is written, "*For your sake we encounter death all day long; we were considered as sheep to be slaughtered.*" 37 No, in all these things we have complete victory through him who loved us! 38 For I am convinced that neither death, nor life, nor angels, nor heavenly rulers, nor things that are present, nor things to come, nor powers, 39 nor height, nor depth, nor anything else in creation will be able to separate us from the love of God in Christ Jesus our LORD.

FRIDAY

Romans 15:7–9

Receive one another, then, just as Christ also received you, to God's glory. 8 For I tell you that Christ has become a servant of the circumcised on behalf of God's truth to confirm the promises made to the fathers,9 and thus the Gentiles glorify God for his mercy. As it is written, "*Because of this I will confess you among the Gentiles, and I will sing praises to your name.*"

MONDAY

Read:
John 3:16–17; Colossians 1:11–14; Hebrews 2:14–15
SOAP:
Colossians 1:13

1. Write out today's **SCRIPTURE** passage.

_____

_____

_____

_____

_____

_____

_____

_____

_____

2. On the blank page to the right, **DRAW** or **WRITE** what this passage means to you.

3. My **PRAYER** for today:

_____

_____

_____

_____

_____

TUESDAY

Read:
Romans 5:8–10; Ephesians 2:1–5

SOAP:
Ephesians 2:4–5

1. Write out today's **SCRIPTURE** passage.

_____

_____

_____

_____

_____

_____

_____

_____

_____

_____

_____

2. On the blank page to the right, **DRAW** or **WRITE** what this passage means to you.

3. My **PRAYER** for today:

_____

_____

_____

_____

_____

_____

WEDNESDAY

John 8:36; 2 Corinthians 3:17

SOAP:
John 8:36

1. Write out today's **SCRIPTURE** passage.

_____

_____

_____

_____

_____

_____

_____

_____

_____

_____

2. On the blank page to the right, **DRAW** or **WRITE** what this passage means to you.

3. My **PRAYER** for today:

_____

_____

_____

_____

_____

_____

THURSDAY

1. Write out today's **SCRIPTURE** passage.

_____

_____

_____

_____

_____

_____

_____

_____

_____

_____

2. On the blank page to the right, **DRAW** or **WRITE** what this passage means to you.

3. My **PRAYER** for today:

_____

_____

_____

_____

_____

FRIDAY

Read:
Romans 15:7–9

SOAP:
Romans 15:7

1. Write out today's **SCRIPTURE** passage.

_____

_____

_____

_____

_____

_____

_____

_____

_____

_____

_____

2. On the blank page to the right, **DRAW** or **WRITE** what this passage means to you.

3. My **PRAYER** for today:

_____

_____

_____

_____

_____

THIS WEEK I LEARNED...

USE THE SPACE BELOW TO DRAW A PICTURE OR WRITE ABOUT WHAT YOU LEARNED THIS WEEK FROM YOUR TIME IN GOD'S WORD.

PRAYER TIME

IT'S IMPORTANT TO PRAY FOR OTHERS. WRITE A PRAYER TO GOD FOR A FRIEND OR A FAMILY MEMBER.

....

....

....

....

....

....

....

....

PRAYER

WRITE DOWN YOUR PRAYER REQUESTS
AND PRAISES FOR EACH DAY.

Prayer focus for this week:
Spend time praying for your friends.

MONDAY

TUESDAY

WEDNESDAY

THURSDAY

FRIDAY

WEEK 3

But our citizenship is in heaven—
and we also eagerly await a savior
from there, the Lord Jesus Christ,

Philippians 3:20

_____

SCRIPTURE FOR WEEK 3

MONDAY

Ephesians 1:5–6

He did this by predestining us to adoption as his legal heirs through Jesus Christ, according to the pleasure of his will— 6 to the praise of the glory of his grace that he has freely bestowed on us in his dearly loved Son.

Colossians 1:12–13

giving thanks to the Father who has qualified you to share in the saints' inheritance in the light. 13 He delivered us from the power of darkness and transferred us to the kingdom of the Son he loves,

TUESDAY

John 1:12

But to all who have received him—those who believe in his name—he has given the right to become God's children

1 John 3:1–2

See what sort of love the Father has given to us: that we should be called God's children— and indeed we are! For this reason the world does not know us: because it did not know him. 2 Dear friends, we are God's children now, and what we will be has not yet been revealed. We know that whenever it is revealed we will be like him, because we will see him just as he is.

WEDNESDAY

Ephesians 1:4

For he chose us in Christ before the foundation of the world that we should be holy and blameless before him in love.

1 Peter 2:9

But you are *a chosen race, a royal priesthood, a holy nation, a people of his own*, so that you may *proclaim the virtues* of the one who called you out of darkness into his marvelous light.

THURSDAY

Ephesians 2:19

So then you are no longer foreigners and noncitizens, but you are fellow citizens with the saints and members of God's household,

Philippians 3:20

But our citizenship is in heaven—and we also eagerly await a savior from there, the LORD Jesus Christ,

FRIDAY

Psalm 139:1–3

O LORD, you examine me and know me.
2 You know when I sit down and when I get up;
even from far away you understand my motives.
3 You carefully observe me when I travel or when I lie down to rest;
you are aware of everything I do.

1 Corinthians 8:3

But if someone loves God, he is known by God.

MONDAY

Read:
Ephesians 1:5–6; Colossians 1:12–13

SOAP:
Ephesians 1:5

1. Write out today's **SCRIPTURE** passage.

_____

_____

_____

_____

_____

_____

_____

_____

_____

_____

2. On the blank page to the right, **DRAW** or **WRITE** what this passage means to you.

3. My **PRAYER** for today:

_____

_____

_____

_____

_____

TUESDAY

SOAP:
John 1:12

1. Write out today's **SCRIPTURE** passage.

_____

_____

_____

_____

_____

_____

_____

_____

_____

_____

2. On the blank page to the right, **DRAW** or **WRITE** what this passage means to you.

3. My **PRAYER** for today:

_____

_____

_____

_____

_____

WEDNESDAY

Read:
Ephesians 1:4; 1 Peter 2:9
SOAP:
1 Peter 2:9

1. Write out today's **SCRIPTURE** passage.

_____

_____

_____

_____

_____

_____

_____

_____

_____

2. On the blank page to the right, **DRAW** or **WRITE** what this passage means to you.

3. My **PRAYER** for today:

_____

_____

_____

_____

_____

THURSDAY

Read:
Ephesians 2:19; Philippians 3:20
SOAP:
Philippians 3:20

1. Write out today's **SCRIPTURE** passage.

_____

_____

_____

_____

_____

_____

_____

_____

_____

_____

2. On the blank page to the right, **DRAW** or **WRITE** what this passage means to you.

3. My **PRAYER** for today:

_____

_____

_____

_____

_____

FRIDAY

Read:
Psalm 139:1–3; 1 Corinthians 8:3
SOAP:
Psalm 139:1

1. Write out today's **SCRIPTURE** passage.

_____

_____

_____

_____

_____

_____

_____

_____

_____

_____

2. On the blank page to the right, **DRAW** or **WRITE** what this passage means to you.

3. My **PRAYER** for today:

_____

_____

_____

_____

_____

THIS WEEK I LEARNED...

USE THE SPACE BELOW TO DRAW A PICTURE OR WRITE ABOUT WHAT YOU LEARNED THIS WEEK FROM YOUR TIME IN GOD'S WORD.

UNSCRAMBLE THE LETTERS

UNSCRAMBLE THE LETTERS INTO WORDS.

gifovren
f _ _ _ _ _ _ _

eref
f _ _ _

hoscne
c _ _ _ _ _

vesda
s _ _ _ _

nedityti
i _ _ _ _ _ _ _

vedlo
l _ _ _ _

lbsesde
b _ _ _ _ _ _

wnonk
k _ _ _ _

PRAYER

WRITE DOWN YOUR PRAYER REQUESTS
AND PRAISES FOR EACH DAY.

Prayer focus for this week:
Spend time praying for your church.

MONDAY

TUESDAY

WEDNESDAY

THURSDAY

FRIDAY

WEEK 4

You are from God, little children,
and have conquered them, because
the one who is in you is greater
than the one who is in the world.

1 John 4:4

_____

SCRIPTURE FOR WEEK 4

MONDAY

Psalm 139:13–18

Certainly you made my mind and heart;
you wove me together in my mother's womb.
14 I will give you thanks because your deeds are awesome and amazing.
You knew me thoroughly;
15 my bones were not hidden from you,
when I was made in secret
and sewed together in the depths of the earth.
16 Your eyes saw me when I was inside the womb.
All the days ordained for me
were recorded in your scroll
before one of them came into existence.
17 How difficult it is for me to fathom your thoughts about me, O God!
How vast is their sum total.
18 If I tried to count them,
they would outnumber the grains of sand.
Even if I finished counting them,
I would still have to contend with you.

TUESDAY

Numbers 6:24–26

"The Lord bless you and protect you;
25 The Lord make his face to shine upon you,
and be gracious to you;
26 The Lord lift up his countenance upon you
and give you peace.'"

2 Corinthians 9:8–10

And God is able to make all grace overflow to you so that because you have enough of everything in every way at all times, you will overflow in every good work. 9 Just as it is written, "**He has scattered widely, he has given to the poor; his righteousness remains forever.**" 10 Now God who provides seed for the sower and bread for food will provide and multiply your supply of seed and will cause the harvest of your righteousness to grow.

Ephesians 1:3

Blessed is the God and Father of our LORD Jesus Christ, who has blessed us with every spiritual blessing in the heavenly realms in Christ.

WEDNESDAY

Ephesians 2:10

For we are his creative work, having been created in Christ Jesus for good works that God prepared beforehand so we can do them.

2 Timothy 3:16–17

Every scripture is inspired by God and useful for teaching, for reproof, for correction, and for training in righteousness, 17 that the person dedicated to God may be capable and equipped for every good work.

THURSDAY

1 Corinthians 12:4–11

Now there are different gifts, but the same Spirit. 5 And there are different ministries, but the same LORD. 6 And there are different results, but the same God who produces all of them in everyone. 7 To each person the manifestation of the Spirit is given for the benefit of all. 8 For one person is given through the Spirit the message of wisdom, and another the message of knowledge according to the same Spirit, 9 to another faith by the same Spirit, and to another gifts of healing by the one Spirit, 10 to another performance of miracles, to another prophecy, and to another discernment of spirits, to another different kinds of tongues, and to another the interpretation of tongues. 11 It is one and the same Spirit, distributing as he decides to each person, who produces all these things.

2 Corinthians 12:9

But he said to me, "My grace is enough for you, for my power is made perfect in weakness." So then, I will boast most gladly about my weaknesses, so that the power of Christ may reside in me.

Philippians 4:13

I am able to do all things through the one who strengthens me.

FRIDAY

1 John 4:4

You are from God, little children, and have conquered them, because the one who is in you is greater than the one who is in the world.

MONDAY

Read:
Psalm 139:13–18

SOAP:
Psalm 139:13–14

1. Write out today's **SCRIPTURE** passage.

_____

_____

_____

_____

_____

_____

_____

_____

_____

_____

2. On the blank page to the right, **DRAW** or **WRITE** what this passage means to you.

3. My **PRAYER** for today:

_____

_____

_____

_____

_____

TUESDAY

Read:
Numbers 6:24–26; 2 Corinthians 9:8–10; Ephesians 1:3

SOAP:
Ephesians 1:3

1. Write out today's **SCRIPTURE** passage.

_____

_____

_____

_____

_____

_____

_____

_____

_____

_____

2. On the blank page to the right, **DRAW** or **WRITE** what this passage means to you.

3. My **PRAYER** for today:

_____

_____

_____

_____

WEDNESDAY

Read:
Ephesians 2:10; 2 Timothy 3:16–17
SOAP:
Ephesians 2:10

1. Write out today's **SCRIPTURE** passage.

_____

_____

_____

_____

_____

_____

_____

_____

_____

_____

2. On the blank page to the right, **DRAW** or **WRITE** what this passage means to you.

3. My **PRAYER** for today:

_____

_____

_____

_____

_____

THURSDAY

1 Corinthians 12:4–11; 2 Corinthians 12:9; Philippians 4:13

SOAP:
Philippians 4:13

1. Write out today's **SCRIPTURE** passage.

_____

_____

_____

_____

_____

_____

_____

_____

_____

_____

2. On the blank page to the right, **DRAW** or **WRITE** what this passage means to you.

3. My **PRAYER** for today:

_____

_____

_____

_____

_____

_____

FRIDAY

Read:
1 John 4:4
SOAP:
1 John 4:4

1. Write out today's **SCRIPTURE** passage.

_____

_____

_____

_____

_____

_____

_____

_____

_____

_____

2. On the blank page to the right, **DRAW** or **WRITE** what this passage means to you.

3. My **PRAYER** for today:

_____

_____

_____

_____

_____

THIS WEEK I LEARNED...

USE THE SPACE BELOW TO DRAW A PICTURE OR WRITE ABOUT WHAT YOU LEARNED THIS WEEK FROM YOUR TIME IN GOD'S WORD.

THE AMAZING MAZE

FIND YOUR WAY THROUGH THE MAZE TO THE DIFFERENT VERSES AND LOOK THEM UP IN YOUR BIBLE.

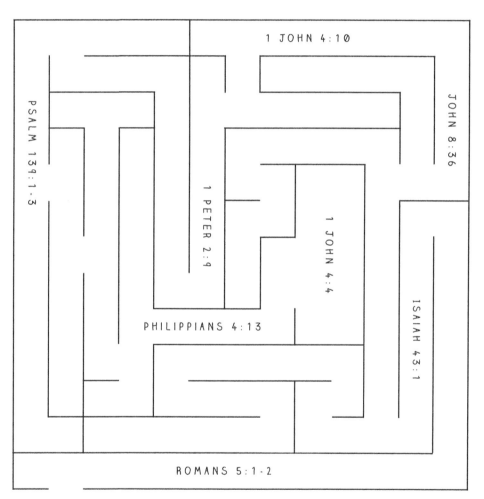

1 JOHN 4:10

JOHN 8:36

PSALM 139:1-3

1 PETER 2:9

1 JOHN 4:4

ISAIAH 43:1

PHILIPPIANS 4:13

ROMANS 5:1-2

START HERE

Made in the USA
Las Vegas, NV
22 October 2024

10068166R00050